Intricate ORNAMENTS

Intricate ORNAMENTS

45 CHRISTMAS DESIGNS TO COLOR

CHUCK ABRAHAM

RP | KIDS
PHILADELPHIA • LONDON

This edition published by Running Press Kids, an imprint of
Running Press Book Publishers
2300 Chestnut Street
Philadelphia, PA 19103-4371

Visit us on the web!
www.runningpress.com

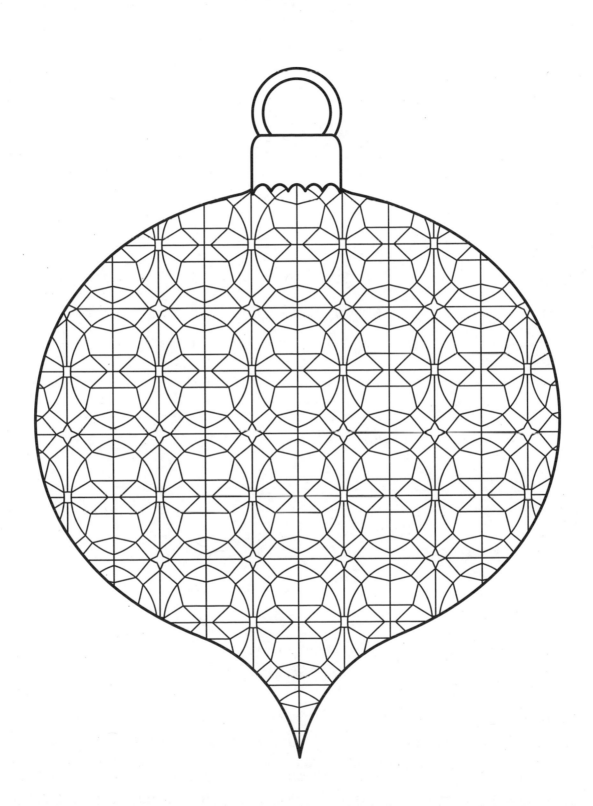

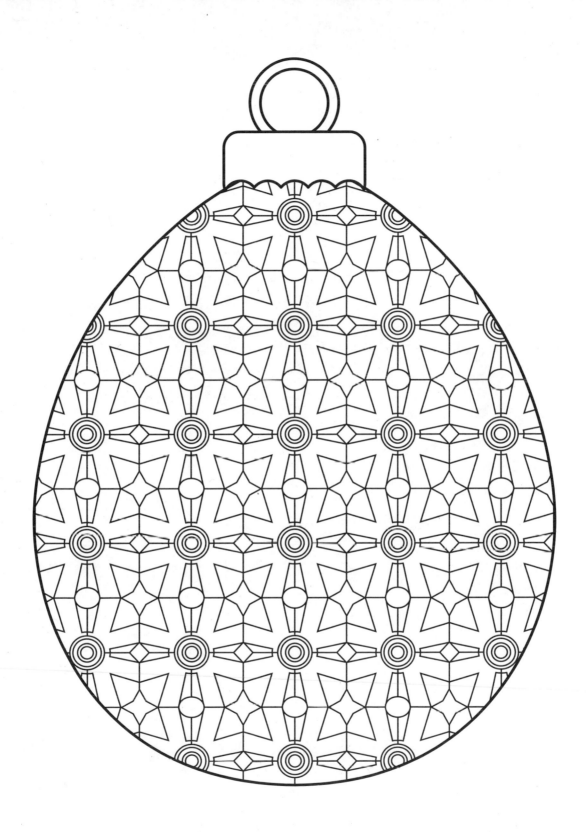

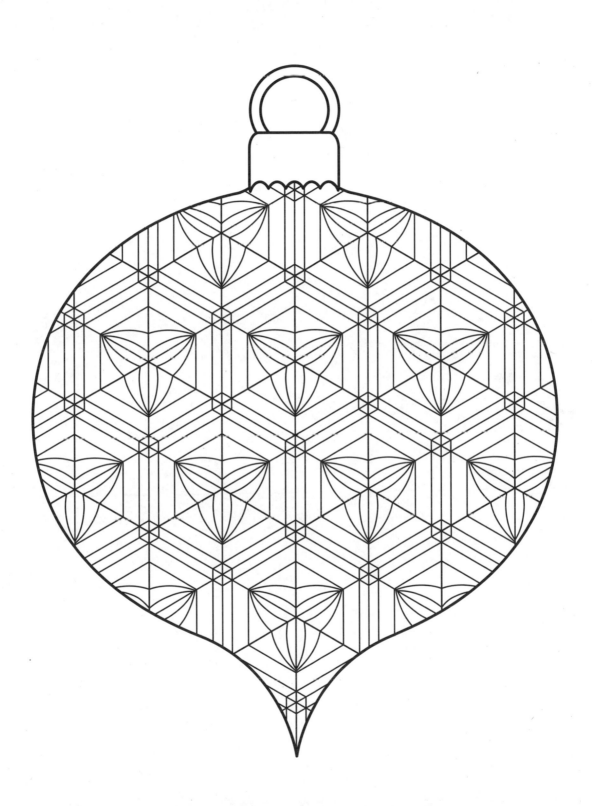

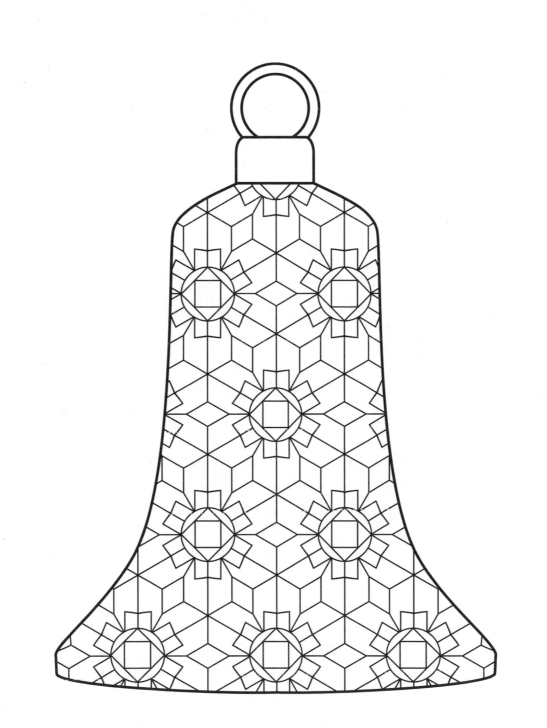

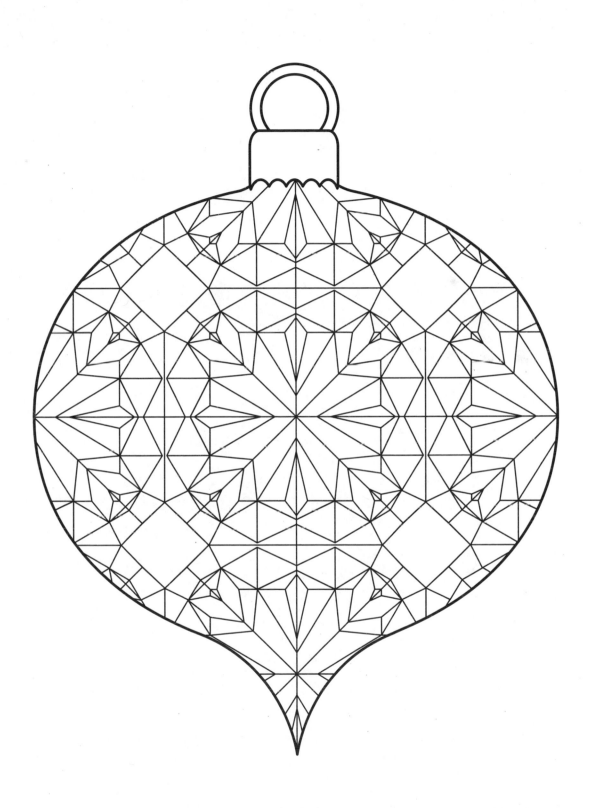

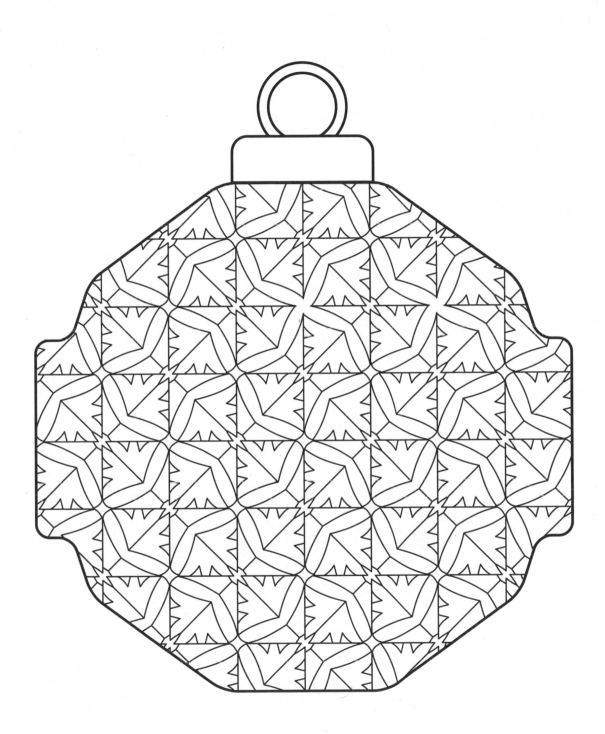

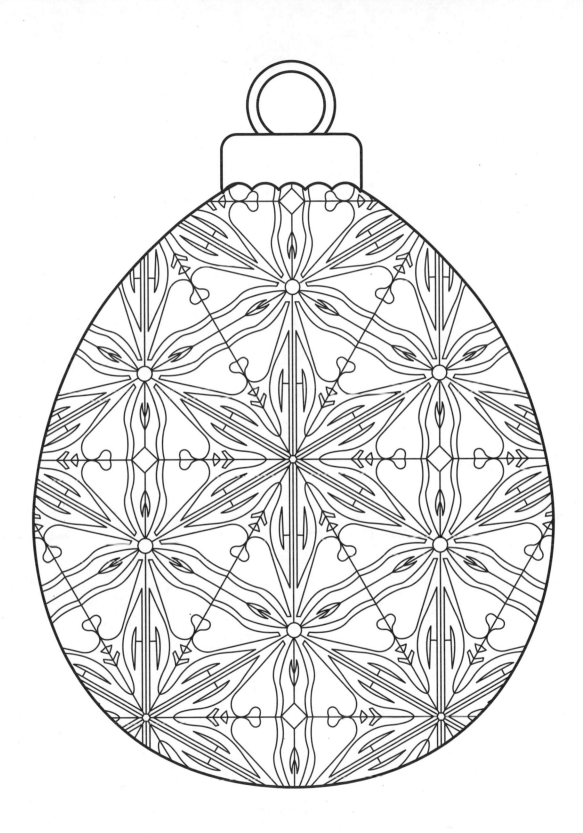